SPIDER-MAN

Discover the incredible world of the
web-slinging super hero—Spider-Man!

•

Meet Spider-Man's closest friends and most evil
adversaries including the Green Goblin and
Dr Octopus!

•

Create your own web-shooting, wall-crawling
Spider-man scenes.

FAMILY AND FRIENDS

The bite of a radioactive spider during a lab experiment turned shy science student Peter Parker into the web-slinging, wall-crawling Spider-Man. Suddenly possessing incredible powers was hard for Peter to deal with, but his Uncle Ben and Aunt May and high-school friends like Flash Thompson helped him get used to being a super hero. As Peter's confidence grew, he plucked up the courage to date girls he wouldn't even have dared speak to before. He also met Mary Jane Watson, the love of his life!

Peter Parker
In high school, Peter was teased by the other students for his bookish ways. All that changed when he became the amazing Spider-Man.

To the Rescue
Mary Jane realized that having Spider-Man for a boyfriend could be a high-risk business.

Mary Jane
She was fun-loving and popular—unlike Peter Parker. She pretended she felt nothing for him—but was there when he needed her.

Aunt May and Uncle Ben
Peter's parents were killed in a plane crash and he was raised by his kindly uncle and aunt. They treated Peter like their own son.

Flash Thompson
Football star Flash used to bully Peter in high school, but the two become close friends as students at Empire State University.

Harry Osborn
At first Peter disliked rich kid Harry, but they became good friends. Peter had no idea that Harry's father was the evil Green Goblin!

Peter's Girlfriends
Peter dated some great girls, including Betty Bryant, Liz Allen, Gwen Stacy and Debra Whitman. However, his secret life as a crime fighter always spoiled things.

SPIDER-SKILLS

Spider-man has all the abilities of a real spider—and then some! He can crawl up walls in a flash, and possesses superhuman strength and agility. Using his scientific knowledge Peter created his own web that shoots out from two devices on his wrists. The web has a myriad uses—a swinging line, a safety net, gliding wings, even a fireproof shield. Peter also has an uncanny ability to detect danger that he calls "Spider-Sense."

Agility
Superb balance, speed and skill allow Spidey to jump, swing, and swoop like the greatest acrobat in the world.

Wall-Crawling
Spidey's hands and feet cling to any surface, enabling him to surprise the bad guys by racing up a wall or skittering across a ceiling.

Alien Costume
Spider-Man's new black suit could change its look and supply endless webbing. However the costume was really an alien being.

Web-Slinging
Two quick taps on the trigger in his palm activate Spider-Man's web-shooters.

Spider-Sense
A strange tingling feeling at the back of his head tells Peter Parker that trouble's in the air. Few villains ever sneak up on him.

The Spider-Mobile
Spider-Man's car had a Spider-Signal device, automatic web-shooters and a seat ejector. Unfortunately, he crashed the car in the Hudson River.

Weightlifting
Spider-Man may not be the strongest hero, but he can easily lift several times his own weight.

FEARSOME FOES

No super hero has ever battled a creepier collection of criminals than Spider-Man. These monsters started out as more-or-less normal human beings but, by design or by strange twists of fate, each one has developed a terrifying superpower, such as crushing tentacles, mutating limbs or electrostatic blasts... Fortunately, Spidey always manages to outwit these super-villains and entangle them in his web. No wonder he's top of their hit list!

Doctor Octopus
Power-crazed scientist Otto Octavius created a terrifying tentacle harness for himself. In time, this contraption merged with his body!

The Green Goblin
Norman Osborn terrified New York City with his weird costume. His Goblin Glider was fitted with an arsenal of weapons.

The Hobgoblin
The menacing Hobgoblin took over from Green Goblin as Spidey's most dangerous enemy. His gauntlets give electric shocks.

Electro
He's a human dynamo delivering blasts of electric power. To defeat him, Spidey has to keep airborne to avoid shattering shocks .

Hydro Man
A freak accident turned sailor Morris Bench into Hydro-Man. This criminal can hide in a puddle or pool, and fire powerful jets of water from his body.

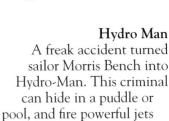

The Sandman
William Baker became the Sandman when his body fused with radioactive sand. Now he can take on any form he wishes.

The Scorpion
This hit-man is twice as strong as Spider-Man. His spiky metal tail is a whip and fires energy blasts and his hands are equipped with powerful pincers.

HEROIC ALLIES

Spider-Man doesn't always have to tackle super-powered villains on his wise-cracking, web-slinging, wall-crawling ownsome. From time to time, other heroes from the Marvel Universe have become his allies, forming devastating partnerships to fight crime. However heroes can be sensitive, touchy types with sizeable egos—a little disagreement over tactics or a harmless jibe and heroic partners may end up fighting each other, instead of the bad guys!

Dr. Strange
When Spidey has supernatural menaces to fight, he can call on Dr. Strange for a paranormal helping hand.

Wolverine
The famous X-Men hero with his adamantium claws is even more of an outsider than Spider-Man. But working together, they're an unbeatable team.

Captain America
The supremo of the Avengers team likes to be the boss and thinks Spidey is too easy-going to be a true hero.

Spider Woman
Julia Carpenter volunteered to be injected with a serum that gave her spider-powers. She became a super hero under government control.

The Incredible Hulk
The green powerhouse is easily annoyed by Spidey's jokes. When the Hulk gets angry, Spider-Man gets going.

X-MEN

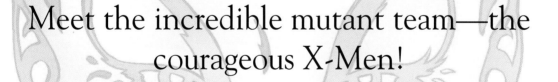

Meet the incredible mutant team—the
courageous X-Men!

•

Learn about the X-Men's amazing mutant
powers and their fight to protect humanity.

•

Use the easy-peel stickers to create your own
action-packed X-Men scenes.

The Original X-Men

The X-Men are mutants, a new type of human with an amazing "extra" ability that normal people lack. Cyclops, Jean Grey, Beast, Angel, and Iceman were the first students to be trained by the mutant genius Professor Xavier, who taught them to use their powers for the good of all humanity.

Blackbird Jet
The X-Men fly into action in their Blackbird jet, a long-distance aircraft capable of flying at four times the speed of sound.

Professor Xavier
The X-Men's founder and leader is Charles Xavier. He is the world's most powerful telepath. His legs were crippled in a battle against an evil alien adversary.

Cyclops
Cyclops wears a special visor to control the powerful force beams emitted by his eyes. The deputy leader of the X-Men, Cyclops' real name is Scott Summers. He was the first member of the X-Men to be recruited by Professor Xavier.

Jean Grey
Jean Grey's powers enable her to read minds and levitate objects. She was originally code-named Marvel Girl, but adopted the name of Phoenix after an encounter with the mysterious Phoenix Force.

Beast
Henry McCoy's ape-like agility earned him his nickname of "the Beast." A brilliant scientist, he later transformed into a fur-covered, animal form.

Angel
The winged mutant Angel is able to fly like a bird. In addition to joining the X-Men, Angel also established his own super hero team, the Champions, in Los Angeles.

Iceman
Bobby Drake is named Iceman as he has the ability to transform his body into ice. He can also freeze moisture in the air to create objects such as bats, shields, and slides.

✕ The New X-Men

Professor Xavier traveled the world to create a new, international team of mutants when the original X-Men were held prisoner by Krakoa, the Living Island. The newcomers succeeded in freeing the team and later replaced many of the original X-Men, who left Xavier's school to pursue their own destinies.

Nightcrawler
Demon-like Nightcrawler can teleport at will and he is also an incredible acrobat. His real name is Kurt Wagner.

Colossus
The giant Russian Piotr Nikolaievitch Rasputin can transform his huge body into organic steel. Virtually invulnerable, he has superhuman strength and can lift over 100 tonnes.

Rogue
When Rogue's skin touches that of another person, she absorbs all of their memories and abilities. However, she cannot control this ability and has to be wary of accidental contact.

Wolverine
Wolverine is a fearsome fighter, with retractable claws and a skeleton made unbreakable by bonded molecules of adamantium alloy. He also has rapid healing powers.

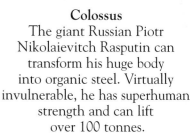

Thunderbird
John Proudstar was a warrior, like his Apache ancestors. Endowed with superhuman strength, he died preventing the escape of the X-Men's enemy, Nefaria.

Storm
Storm has the ability to control the weather around her. She can also create rain, hail, snow, fog, and lightning on demand.

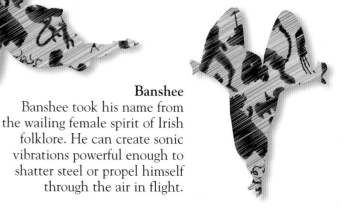

Havoc
Alex Summers—the brother of Cyclops—was named Havoc because of his ability to discharge powerful, destructive waves of force and heat.

Banshee
Banshee took his name from the wailing female spirit of Irish folklore. He can create sonic vibrations powerful enough to shatter steel or propel himself through the air in flight.

⊗ The X-Men's Enemies

Many of the X-Men's adversaries are evil or misguided mutants. They consider themselves to be superior to normal humans and seek to destroy or enslave humanity and its protectors—the X-Men. Despite their awesome powers and weapons, these deadly foes are no match for Professor Xavier's heroic team.

Sabretooth
The mutant predator Sabretooth sees humanity as prey for him to hunt, fight, and kill. He has superhuman senses and ferocious fighting abilities.

Juggernaut
Sustained by mystical forces, Juggernaut has vast physical strength. When he starts moving, he is virtually unstoppable.

Sentinel
The Sentinels are immense robots designed to hunt down mutants. They are equipped with electron beam guns, plasma guns, and lasers. Some Sentinels can spray liquid nitrogen from their eyes.

Apocalypse
Apocalypse is endowed with incredible strength and an amazingly long lifespan. He can also transform any part of his body into a living weapon.

Nemesis
A mutant from an alternate reality, Nemesis feeds off his victims' life forces, which enables him to release enough energy to devastate a planet.

Magneto
Magneto can control magnetism and other electromagnetic forces. He believes mutants will only be free if they enslave the rest of the human race.

Lady Deathstrike
A lethal cyborg, Lady Deathstrike has metal claws for fingers and a skeleton laced with adamantium alloy. She has a particular grudge against Wolverine.

⊗ *Aliens and Outcasts*

The X-Men have encountered several alien races throughout their history, many of whom have posed a threat to the security of the Earth. Colossus's brother, Mikhail Rasputin, also became a danger when he lead an outcast group of mutants called the Morlocks in a war against humankind.

Acanti
These whale-like sentient beings can travel through space at extraordinary speeds. Many Acanti have been enslaved by the Brood.

Brood
Cunning, vicious hunters, the Brood are insect-like creatures driven by their need to breed.

Mikhail Rasputin
Mikhail's powers enable him to channel any form of energy and to alter the molecular structure of matter. He was once a cosmonaut in the Russian space program.

Shi'ar
The Shi'ar are an alien race with both bird- and mammal-like characteristics. They rule a vast empire that extends throughout the galaxy.

Sidri
The Sidri are formidable creatures that live in deep space. They are covered in organic body armor and can fire force blasts from their bodies.

FANTASTIC FOUR

Enter the exciting world of the Fantastic Four and learn about their most thrilling adventures!

•

Find out fascinating facts about the Fantastic Four and all their friends and foes.

•

Create your own action scenes with your favorite Fantastic Four characters.

The Transformation

When four friends—Reed Richards, Ben Grimm, Sue Storm, and her brother Johnny—journeyed into outer space, their lives were changed forever. They were all exposed to dangerous levels of radiation that genetically altered them and gave them superhuman powers. From that day on the four friends had new identities as Mr. Fantastic, the Thing, the Invisible Woman, and the Human Torch. Together, they formed the Fantastic Four.

NO TURNING BACK

Traveling in Reed's starship, the four friends passed through an area of intense cosmic energy called the Van Allen belt. They were exposed to high levels of radiation.

WHERE IT ALL BEGAN

After college, Reed Richards worked as an aeronautical engineer. He spent his inheritance building and launching this starship.

INVISIBLE WOMAN

Sue Storm gained the ability to bend rays of light to make herself and other objects invisible!

MR. FANTASTIC

Reed became Mr. Fantastic. He could stretch, expand, or compress himself into any shape imaginable.

THE THING

The cosmic rays in outer space caused Ben Grimm's muscles, bones, internal organs, and skin to become tough and dense. That's why he looks like he's made of rock.

HUMAN TORCH

Johnny Storm developed the amazing ability to transform his body into a living flame upon command.

THE FANTASTIC FOUR

With their new super powers, the friends formed the Fantastic Four—a team of Super Heroes unlike any other.

Mr Fantastic and Invisible Woman

Mr. Fantastic and the Invisible Woman are superhuman, celebrity adventurers. Known around the world for his scientific genius, Reed is the natural leader of the Fantastic Four. Sue, his wife, has incredible powers. She can make anything invisible and create force fields that protect the Fantastic Four when they get into trouble. Their exciting adventures make the world a better and safer place for everyone including their two children, Franklin and Valeria.

THE BAXTER BUILDING

From the outside this looks like an ordinary office building, but it is actually the high-tech headquarters of the Fantastic Four.

INVENTIONS

Reed's scientific inventions include ray guns, teleportation devices, and multi-purpose vehicles. This car can fly at the speed of light.

GENIUS

Reed has cracked formulas and codes that other scientists have failed to work out for centuries. He has also discovered other dimensions that no one knew existed.

PSIONIC FORCE

Sue's brain cells produce psionic energy, which means that she can create force fields to protect herself and others.

CARING FATHER

Although Reed is busy solving the world's scientific problems, he makes time to care for and protect his family.

FORCE FIELDS

By projecting force fields beneath her, Sue appears to fly through the air.

SUPER PARENTS

When Franklin's parents come back from a trip, they bring him souvenirs like meteorites instead of t-shirts.

A UNIQUE TEAM

The Fantastic Four are "imaginauts"—astronauts and explorers, not street patrolling crime-fighters like other Super Heroes.

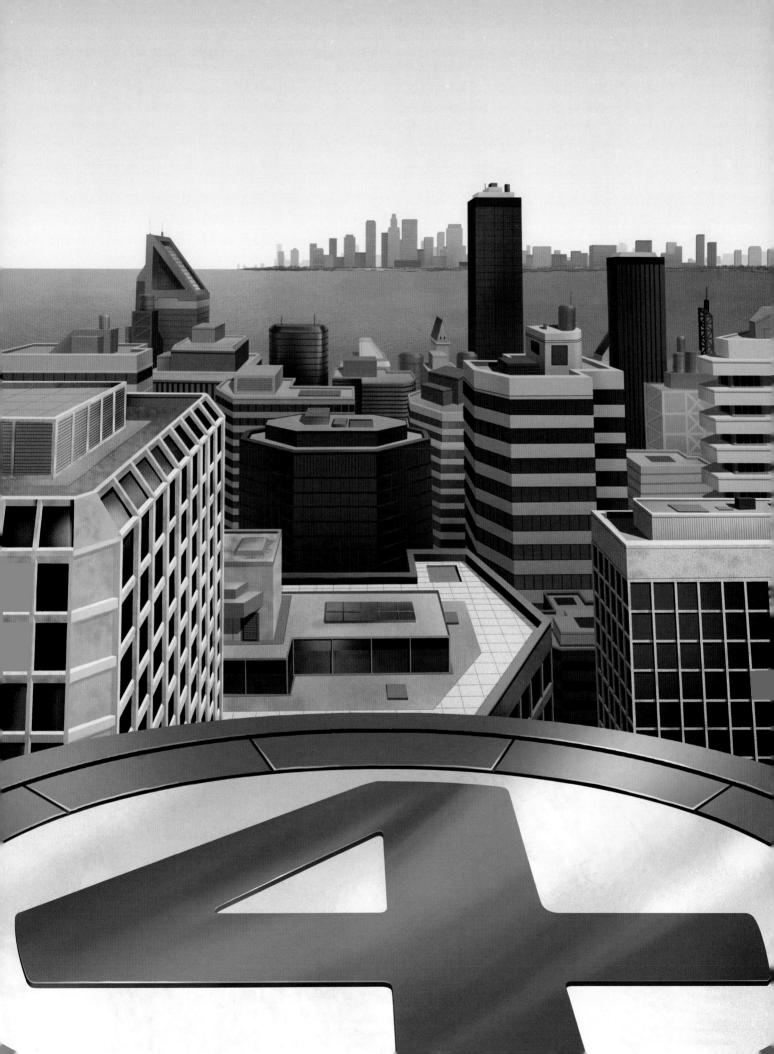

Human Torch and Thing

The Torch is the hothead of the Fantastic Four. He takes advantage of the Thing's good nature and torments him at every chance. The Thing's thick skin protects him from bullets and fire, but not from the Torch's teasing! The Thing sometimes plays pranks on the Torch as well, but, despite their bickering, deep down they're the best of friends.

FIREPROOF WARDROBE
Johnny's clothes are made of unstable molecules. This means he can "flame on" without burning all his clothes off!

Flame on!

FIRE FLY
The Torch's flame form is lighter than air, which allows him to fly.

GREAT BALLS OF FIRE!
The Torch can throw bolts of fire of all sizes, from small fire balls to super-charged nova blasts.

Tougher than a brick wall

INDESTRUCTIBLE!
The Thing's rock-hard skin can survive extreme temperatures and armor-piercing bazooka shells.

SUPER STRONG
Evil villains watch out! The Thing has greater strength and endurance than almost anything else on earth.

UNCLE BEN
Underneath his tough shell, the Thing is a really caring guy. Both Franklin and Val love playing with their "Uncle Ben."

Doctor Doom

Victor Von Doom was raised by gypsies in Latveria after both his parents died when he was young. His anger at losing his parents made him hate the whole world. He vowed to learn everything he could to make him powerful and make the world suffer for his loss. When Doom met Reed Richards at university, Doom quickly became jealous of Reed's intelligence and the two became bitter rivals.

RULER OF LATVERIA

Doom's quest for power led him to become the ruler of Latveria. Of course, his real goal is to rule the world! If Doom can destroy the Fantastic Four, this just might happen.

GIFTED STUDENT

Like the young Reed Richards, Victor Von Doom was a highly gifted student. Doom met Reed at State University in New York when they were both young scientists.

THE MASKED MAN

Doom was so vain that he couldn't bear his scarred face after the accident. He had a metal mask made to conceal his face, but he put it on before it had cooled and was disfigured forever.

FATAL MISTAKE

Victor was a talented but arrogant scientist. He was determined to carry out an illegal experiment even though Reed warned him that the calculations were incorrect. The experiment went wrong and left Doom with a scar on his face, for which he blamed Reed.

SCIENTIST AND SORCERER

Doom has great scientific knowledge, but he is also a powerful sorcerer.

Meet Earth's mightiest team—the
superhuman Avengers!

•

Learn about the Avengers' amazing abilities
and their most dramatic battles.

•

Create your own action-packed
Avengers scenes.

 # TEAM OF MIGHT

The *Avengers are Earth's* mightiest superhuman team, formed to combat threats that are too powerful for any single hero to take on. The team was born when Thor, Iron Man, Ant-Man and Wasp joined to thwart the wily wizardry of the Norse trickster god Loki, who was stirring up trouble between his foster brother Thor and the rampaging Hulk. Eventually they defeated Loki's scheming and the heroic band decided to call themselves the Avengers.

THOR
Thor is the Norse god of Thunder. He wields a magical hammer named Mjolnir that projects lightning blasts and enables him to fly.

CAPTAIN AMERICA
This famous hero was missing believed dead, until the team found him frozen in the Arctic. He soon recovered to become the leader of the Avengers.

IRON MAN
Billionaire inventor Tony Stark wears a battlesuit equipped with jet-powered boots and repulsor blasters. His New York mansion is the Avengers' base.

THE WASP
Janet Van Dyne became Ant-Man's crimebusting partner She can shrink in size, grow wasp wings and communicate with insects thanks to Henry Pym's scientific genius.

ANT-MAN
Scientist Henry Pym invented a serum that shrank him to insect size. His helmet enabled him to communicate with ants, who became his allies.

HULK
He is superstrong, invulnerable and incredibly fast. However, the Hulk was only an Avenger for a short time before his bad temper got the better of him.

GIANT-MAN
Henry Pym found that being an ant-sized hero had its drawbacks, so he turned himself into Giant-Man, superhuman in size and strength.

AVENGERS ASSEMBLE!

Keeping a team of heroes together is no easy task. Superpowered superhumans, however well-intentioned, often have super-sized egos to match and don't always pull in the same direction. Heroes also tend to have many demands on their time and can't always be available. So, over the years, the Avengers team has gone through many intriguing and exciting changes of personnel, enabling new heroes with new powers to answer the inspiring rallying call: "Avengers assemble!"

THE VISION
This android was programmed with human emotions by the evil Ultron to destroy the Avengers. Instead, the Vision joined them.

SCARLET WITCH
Wanda Maximoff possesses powerful magical abilities called hex power. She was once married to Vision.

FALCON
Soaring on jet-powered glider wings, Falcon is a close ally of Captain America and a protector of the people of Harlem in New York City.

QUICKSILVER
Pietro Maximoff possesses superhuman speed—and often rushes in when wiser heroes would be more careful. His sister Wanda is the magic-wielding Scarlet Witch.

SHE-HULK
Jennifer Walters is the cousin of Bruce Banner, the Hulk. Like him she has superhuman strength and endurance; however she is better at anger management!

JACK OF HEARTS
As a boy, Jack Hart was drenched with a fuel called "Zero Liquid." His body is now filled with explosive energy.

NAMOR
The arrogant monarch of the undersea realm of Atlantis sometimes aids the Avengers. He is superhumanly strong, can breathe underwater, and also fly.

HAWKEYE
With his trick arrows and deadly aim, Hawkeye has served the team well—despite his rebel stance.

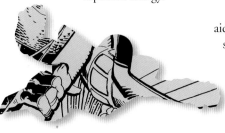

ⓐ SUPER-VILLAIN GALLERY

The chief enemies of the Avengers are no ordinary villains—they are ruthless alien conquerors or godlike mischief-makers possessing weapons of mass destruction, vast armies or awesome magical powers. Only the Avengers, working as a team, can stop them bringing chaos and terror to the world.

THANOS
This exile from Saturn's moon Titan has slaughtered millions. He is determined to wipe out all life in the hope that the supernatural being Death will return his love. His hands project powerful energy blasts.

LOKI
The trickster god from Asgard is Thor's half-brother and a master magician. Loki is one of the Avengers' most frequent and most cunning enemies.

EXECUTIONER
Skurge is from the Norse realm of Asgard. As the hugely strong—but not overly intelligent—Executioner, he frequently aided Enchantress in her various plots. After all, he was totally in love with her.

SUPER-SKRULL
This deadly enemy needs no weapons—he has all the powers of the Fantastic Four, including elasticity, fire projection, invisibility and super-strength.

KANG
Kang is obsessed with conquest and travels back and forth through time seeking to dominate the world in every single historical era—including this one!

ENCHANTRESS
This seductive sorceress schemes to win power for herself and also the heart of Thor, ruler of Asgard, home of the Norse gods. A single kiss from the Enchantress' lips will make any man do her bidding for at least a week.

ULTRON
This "living machine" started out as a scientific experiment by Hank Pym, but took on a life of its own and ran way out of control. Ultron hates Pym, the Avengers team and the whole of humanity.

Stickers

Dr Octopus

Spider-Man

Dr Strange

Hulk

Spider-Man

Spider-Man

Harry
Osborn

Spider-Man

Kraven
the Hunter

Green
Goblin

Mary Jane and
Spider-Man

Spider-Mobile

Kaine

Stickers

Aunt May and Uncle Ben

Spidey v. Molten Man

Spider-Man

Spider-Man and heroes

Spider-Man

Green Goblin

Wolverine

Spider-Woman

Spider-Man

Spider-Man

Peter Parker

Spider-Man

Spider-Man

Spider-Man

Spider-Man

STICKERS

Wolverine

Professor Xavier

Thunderbird

Wolverine

Storm

Rogue

Shi'ar

Havoc

Wolverine

Acanti

Cyclops

Rogue

STICKERS

Iceman

Bishop

Colossus

Mystique

Nightcrawler

Wolverine

Banshee

Sentinel

Magneto

Sabretooth

Juggernaut

Gambit

Stickers

Reed Richards

Sue Richards

Johnny Storm

Ben Grimm

Inventions

No turning back

The Torch

Fatal mistake

The Fantastic Four

Gifted student

Scientist and sorcerer

Stickers

Fantastic
Four

Force fields

Super parents

Mr. Fantastic

Fireproof
wardrobe

Ruler of
Latveria

Stickers

Dr. Doom fights Captain America

Beast

Wasp

Baron Zemo

Scarlet Witch

Thanos

Wasp

Vision fights Ultron

Super-Skrull

Quicksilver

Hulk

Giant-Man

Egghead

Iron Man fights Temugin

Stickers

Captain America

Thor

Avengers' Quinjet

Ant-Man

Falcon

She-Hulk

Namor

Kang

Ant-Man

Namor

S.H.I.E.L.D. aircraft carrier

Order

Black Panther

Captain America

Vision

Stickers

Ultron

Black Widow

Thor logo

Black Knight

Warbird

Iron Man

Captain Britain

Avengers' Quinjet

She-Hulk fights horse monster

Loki

Thor

KRROOOM

Nighthawk

Spider-Woman

Hawkeye

Enchantress

Executioner

Stickers

Namor
fights Hulk

Black
Widow

Jack of Hearts

Scarlet
Witch

Iron Man

The Falcon

Spider-Woman

S.H.I.E.L.D
jet fighter

Thor

Captain America
fights Kang

The Vision

Sentinel

Iron Man

Hawkeye

Spider-Man

Avengers
logo

Jack of
Hearts

Stickers

A unique team

Caring father

Uncle Ben

Where it all began

The masked man

Super strong

Genius

Stickers

Invisible Woman

Baxter Building

Fire fly

Indestructible

Reed Richards   Sue Richards   Johnny Storm   Ben Grimm

FANTASTIC FOUR

The Thing

Flame on!

STICKERS

Angel

Beast

Blackbird Jet

Shadowcat

Jean Grey

Wolverine

Nemesis

Beast

Magneto

Apocalypse

Cyclops

Lady Deathstrike

Cyclops

Colossus

STICKERS

Sidri

Iceman

Cyclops

Shadowcat

Professor Xavier

Brood

Psylocke

Beast

Magneto

Nightcrawler

Mikhail Rasputin

Storm

Wolverine

Stickers

Alien Costume

Spider-Man

Peter Parker's girlfriends

Electro

Spider-Man

Captain America

Peter Parker

Kingpin

Scorpion

Spider-Man

Hydro-Man

Silver Sable

Spider-Man

Spider-Man

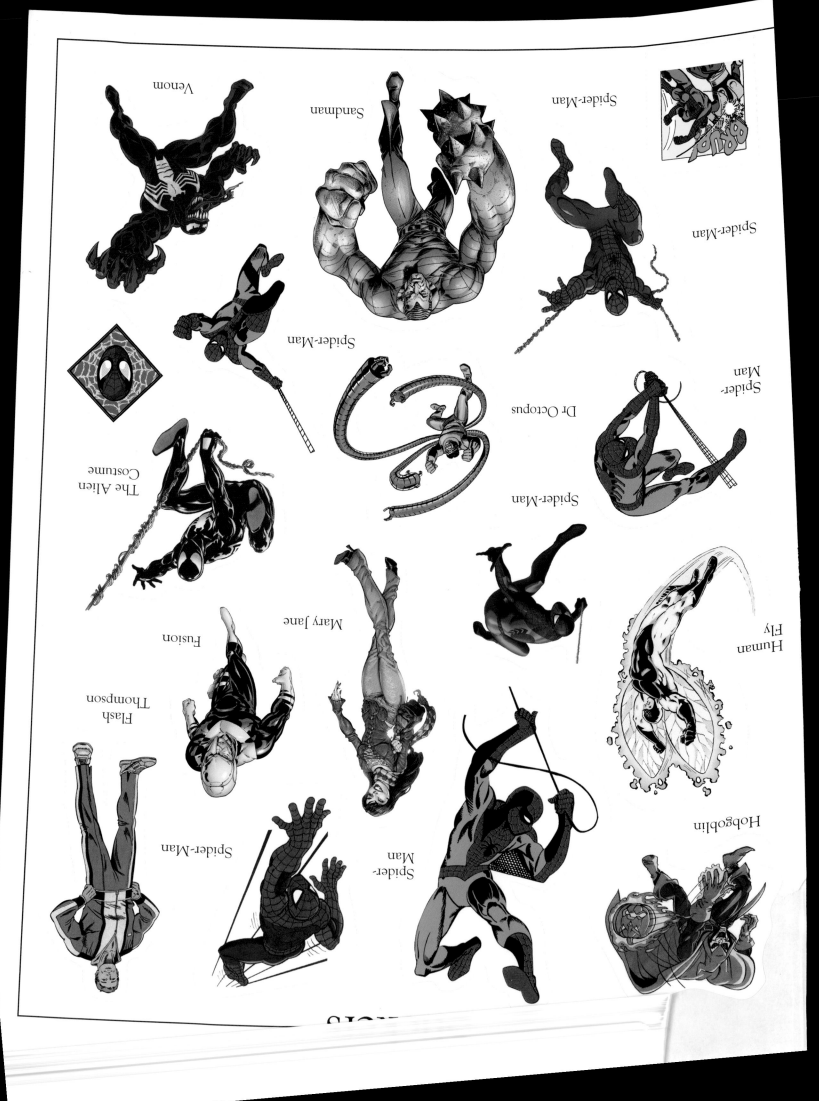